SLOWGIRL

BY GREG PIERCE

DRAMATISTS
PLAY SERVICE
INC.

SLOWGIRL
Copyright © 2013, Greg Pierce

All Rights Reserved

CAUTION: Professionals and amateurs are hereby warned that performance of SLOWGIRL is subject to payment of a royalty. It is fully protected under the copyright laws of the United States of America, and of all countries covered by the International Copyright Union (including the Dominion of Canada and the rest of the British Commonwealth), and of all countries covered by the Pan-American Copyright Convention, the Universal Copyright Convention, the Berne Convention, and of all countries with which the United States has reciprocal copyright relations. All rights, including without limitation professional/amateur stage rights, motion picture, recitation, lecturing, public reading, radio broadcasting, television, video or sound recording, all other forms of mechanical, electronic and digital reproduction, transmission and distribution, such as CD, DVD, the Internet, private and file-sharing networks, information storage and retrieval systems, photocopying, and the rights of translation into foreign languages are strictly reserved. Particular emphasis is placed upon the matter of readings, permission for which must be secured from the Author's agent in writing.

The English language stock and amateur stage performance rights in the United States, its territories, possessions and Canada for SLOWGIRL are controlled exclusively by DRAMATISTS PLAY SERVICE, INC., 440 Park Avenue South, New York, NY 10016. No professional or nonprofessional performance of the Play may be given without obtaining in advance the written permission of DRAMATISTS PLAY SERVICE, INC., and paying the requisite fee.

Inquiries concerning all other rights should be addressed to William Morris Endeavor Entertainment, LLC, 1325 Avenue of the Americas, New York, NY 10019. Attn: Scott Chaloff.

SPECIAL NOTE

Anyone receiving permission to produce SLOWGIRL is required to give credit to the Author as sole and exclusive Author of the Play on the title page of all programs distributed in connection with performances of the Play and in all instances in which the title of the Play appears for purposes of advertising, publicizing or otherwise exploiting the Play and/or a production thereof. The name of the Author must appear on a separate line, in which no other name appears, immediately beneath the title and in size of type equal to 50% of the size of the largest, most prominent letter used for the title of the Play. No person, firm or entity may receive credit larger or more prominent than that accorded the Author. The following acknowledgment must appear on the title page in all programs distributed in connection with performances of the Play:

Produced by Lincoln Center Theater,
New York City, 2012

SLOWGIRL was produced by LCT3/Lincoln Center Theater at the Claire Tow Theater, New York City, 2012. It was directed by Anne Kauffman; the set design was by Rachel Hauck; the costume design was by Emily Rebholz; the lighting was by Japhy Weideman; the sound design was by Leah Gelpe; the stage manager was Charles M. Turner III; the managing director was Adam Siegel; and the production manager was Jeff Hamlin. The cast was as follows:

STERLING .... Željko Ivanek
BECKY .... Sarah Steele

CHARACTERS

BECKY — 17, niece

STERLING — 49, uncle

PLACE

Sterling's house outside the tiny town of Los Angeles, Costa Rica.

TIME

A week in late April.

SCENE BREAKDOWN

Scene 1: Monday afternoon, Sterling's house.
Scene 2: Tuesday afternoon, the walking labyrinth up the hill.
Scene 3: Thursday, the middle of the night, Sterling's house.
Scene 4: Saturday night, Sterling's house.

NOTES

There is no intermission.

Sonia is pronounced SOH-nya.

… means the line trails off.
— means an interruption.
// means the point at which the following line begins.
[ ] means unspoken dialogue.

Sterling's house: He did the best he could with a big slab of concrete, some boards, and a tin roof. There are some New England touches to remind him of home. There's a hammock on the front porch, then a couple steps down to the driveway. The house is always wide open. Inside, we can see a tidy kitchen/living room area and doors to the bedroom and bathroom in back. The bedroom wall goes up about six feet, then stops. Anyone can hear anything in here. It was obviously designed for only one person.

SLOWGIRL

Scene 1

Monday afternoon. Sterling's house.

Sterling is asleep in the hammock on his porch, a Latin American story collection in Spanish spread across his chest. Becky stands there watching him. She's out of her element. Her backpack is so stuffed it looks like it's about to burst. She's not sure whether she should wake him. She goes over to the hammock, hesitates, and then swings it, barely, from the strings just above his head.

BECKY. *(Quietly.)* Uncle Sterling? *(Nothing. She sits down on the steps, takes off her backpack, looks around. It's surreal, being here all of the sudden. Quietly.)* Uncle Sterling? *(Nothing. She hears an unfamiliar bird off in the distance. A little louder.)* Uncle Sterling? *(Sterling wakes up suddenly, stabilizes himself.)*
STERLING. Whoa, hey. You're here.
BECKY. Yeah. Hi.
STERLING. Hey. *(Beat.)* You made good time.
BECKY. Really? I left like nine hours ago.
STERLING. Oh! Right on schedule then. *(Beat. He looks her over.)* So ... Hector picked you up and everything, no problem?
BECKY. Yeah. He's really nice. We didn't have much of a conversation 'cause my Spanish sucks ass.
STERLING. *(Surprised by that.)* Oh ... he knows more English than he lets on. *(Pause. They don't know what to say.)* Well. Welcome. *(He stands up and gives Becky a somewhat mechanical hug.)*
BECKY. Thanks. So this is your place?
STERLING. Yes.

BECKY. Wow. And ... you own all this? *(Re: land.)*
STERLING. Pretty much. I don't own across the road — that's Hector's — from the balsa trees up to the uh ... ridge. *(Is that the right word?)*
BECKY. Whoa. This is so crazy. I'm sorry, it just hit me. I'm in the *jungle.* You live in the *jungle.*
STERLING. Yes, it's weird, isn't it? So ... that folds out. That's where you'll be sleeping but you can always use the bedroom for changing or ... if you need privacy.
BECKY. 'Kay. *(She tosses down her backpack. He gives her the quick tour.)*
STERLING. Bathroom, fresh water — you should brush your teeth with that — flashlights, first aid kit.
BECKY. Where are your doors?
STERLING. They're in the shed. I keep them off in the dry season.
BECKY. So there's no doors at night?
STERLING. No.
BECKY. So stuff can just come in?
STERLING. What do you mean by "stuff"?
BECKY. Like ... animals?
STERLING. They could, I suppose. They don't seem very interested —
BECKY. — So a jaguar could just like, run in here in the middle of the night?
STERLING. I've never seen a jaguar. I've seen a panther.
BECKY. In here??
STERLING. No, no. Way up in the hills — I can put the doors on at night if it'd make you more comfortable ...
BECKY. Whatever, it's fine. *(Looking around.)* Whoa. You live in the *jungle. (Sterling smiles. Pause. Nervously.)* Oh my God, that plane from San Jose's so crazy — there were only like eight of us and one lady was like super-sized — I swear to God I've never been so claustrophobic in my life, I just, like, plastered my face against the window and did this *(Her hands become horse blinders.)* so I couldn't see the edges of the window so I could just pretend there was no plane and I was just floating in the clouds — isn't that weird, how you can do that? I don't know if you're claustrophobic, but I am, really bad, and I figured out that if you can just, like, mindfuck yourself, you can totally survive anything — but it didn't really work this time 'cause there was this skeevy guy who was like, pretending he was so

into the scenery he needed to like, lean over me to get a better look. I was like "How's that scenery, sketchball?" *(Beat.)* It was nasty.
STERLING. Sorry, that sounds unpleasant.
BECKY. Whatever, I'm here. *(Beat.)* Oh, but then we landed and there was like, one dude sitting on his Jeep with a gigantic machete and a pole, and I was like, "That is *not* my ride to Uncle Sterling's ... "
STERLING. Oh. *(Amused.)* Hector loves his sugar cane.
BECKY. It's so gross! He just cuts it off and eats it?
STERLING. Everybody does. Sorry I didn't pick you up ... he's better on those roads.
BECKY. How come his teeth aren't, like, black?
STERLING. I don't know. Did he push any on you?
BECKY. He kept handing me these little chunks but I was like, "No thanks, I had some nuts on the plane." I don't think he understood me. *(Beat.)* Do you remember the last time we saw each other?
STERLING. Um ... I guess it was probably when Karen and I were about to go over to England, right? We came and stayed with you guys for a couple nights? Or was there another ...
BECKY. Nope, that was it. I was eight.
STERLING. Oof ... that's embarrassing.
BECKY. Why?
STERLING. Oh no — I just ... probably should've visited a little more in the last ... nine years.
BECKY. Don't worry 'bout it. 'Member what my mom made us? *(He doesn't.)* Fondue.
STERLING. Oh ... *(Trying to remember.)*
BECKY. Eckh, she was going through her whole fondue thing. Eckh! It makes me wanna puke just thinking about it — fondue's like the nastiest, fattiest, eckh ... and she didn't, like, stir the cheese enough or something so you'd dip your bread cube in and you'd get, like, a big old salty old chunk. Eckh, I can't even talk about this anymore. *(Beat.)* Karen was wearing a jean jacket, right? It had like, whatdoyoucallit, embroidery on the shoulder? ... almost, like, country western-style or something?
STERLING. Wow. You have a good memory.
BECKY. I always remember what people are eating and wearing. I forget names and faces like that *(Snaps.)* but food and clothes ... I guess that means I'm shallow, right?

STERLING. No ... I tend to ... well, I forget most things. *(Beat.)* I have a fruit smoothie in the afternoon. Do you want a fruit smoothie?
BECKY. Sure.
STERLING. Great. *(He gets to work.)* The fruit's from right here on the property. Hector picks it and his wife Sonia cuts it up and puts it in these handy little freezer baggies so I can just ... There's mango, banana, papaya ... Sonia's a fantastic cook too — you'll see. She makes tortillas and guacamole and mashed plantain chips. Have you ever had a mashed —
BECKY. — So what, you pay them like ten cents a day and they do all your work for you?
STERLING. *(Taken aback.)* No. I pay them very fairly. And they only work ...
BECKY. Just kidding, God.
STERLING. Well, I'm very lucky to have them. *(He dumps the frozen fruit into the blender.)* And flowers — Sonia cooks with flowers sometimes.
BECKY. Whoa, weird. *(He takes out a syrup container and starts adding its contents.)* What's that? — It looks like cum.
STERLING. *(Taken aback, again.)* It's a ... sweet, coconut syrup-type-thing. It's very tasty.
BECKY. Gross. Can you just put that in yours?
STERLING. Alright. *(He does. As he blends the smoothie, Becky walks around, checking the place out as though she were window shopping. She stops at his bookshelf.)*
BECKY. You can read Spanish?
STERLING. *(Can't hear over the blender.)* Sorry?
BECKY. You can read Spanish?
STERLING. Yes.
BECKY. Are you like ... fluent?
STERLING. Yes.
BECKY. That was a dumb question — you live here. How long did it take you to get fluent?
STERLING. Two years, maybe?
BECKY. OK, so how do you say, "It took me two years to get fluent in Spanish"?
STERLING. *Esto me tomó dos años para ser fluido en español.*
BECKY. Whoa, cool. Do you speak other languages?
STERLING. German and French. Not fluently though. *(He hands her a smoothie. They sit on the steps.)* Salud.

BECKY. *Salute.* Thanks a lot for having me.
STERLING. Thanks for coming down. *(They drink.)*
BECKY. Do you have any rum?
STERLING. *(Awkwardly.)* I do, but ...
BECKY. That'd go great in here, wouldn't it?
STERLING. It would. *(Beat.)* I'm not sure I should ...
BECKY. Isn't the drinking age like eighteen here?
STERLING. I think so ...
BECKY. I'm gonna be eighteen in like, seven months. *(Sterling doesn't know what to say.)* Whatever, I don't need any rum right now — it'll probly just make me fall asleep.
STERLING. *(Relieved.)* Yes, that happens to me too. It must run in the family. *(They drink.)*
BECKY. So my mom told you what's up, right?
STERLING. She ... not really. She said you were in some trouble.
BECKY. Tch. What else did she say?
STERLING. Uh ... not very much, to be honest. I didn't ask many questions. She mostly told me how important it was for you to get away for a little while and ... She said whatever you wanted to tell me, you'd tell me.
BECKY. *(Scoffs.)* That's so like my mom. She'll say anything to avoid having to have an actual conversation.
STERLING. No, she was very ... [forthcoming.]
BECKY. Whatever, I shouldn't insult her in front of you. I forget, she's your sister.
STERLING. No, I ... that's fine. Becky, I wanted to say ... you don't have to explain anything. This is supposed to be a place for you to get away and ...
BECKY. So this is like ... your Monday? *(Beat.)* What do you do all day?
STERLING. I read. I walk. I build trails.
BECKY. For who? You?
STERLING. Yes, mostly. Sometimes people from the village come and —
BECKY. — Where's the village?
STERLING. Down the hill. Los Angeles. Population eighty-four.
BECKY. You're kidding me.
STERLING. No.
BECKY. It's really called "Los Angeles"?
STERLING. Yes. And San Francisco's up the road the other way.

Population a hundred and thirty, I think?
BECKY. That's hilarious. So are there, like, people for you to hang out with?
STERLING. Uh … there are people around. Everyone's very nice. I wouldn't say I "hang out" with them.
BECKY. So you're basically a loner?
STERLING. Pretty much.
BECKY. That sucks.
STERLING. Well, you don't move to the jungle unless you sort of …
BECKY. I'd probly blow my brains out if I spent all my time alone. *(Sterling can't think of a response.)* I mean, don't you get bored?
STERLING. No.
BECKY. Never?
STERLING. No.
BECKY. I don't believe you.
STERLING. I don't. I get lonely sometimes, but never bored. Do you want some more smoothie?
BECKY. I probly shouldn't — there's like a buttload of sugar in fruit. Whatever … sure. *(He pours.)*
STERLING. Good. You must be hungry too. I'm sorry, I forgot — you probably haven't eaten since —
BECKY. — I'm fine. My stomach still feels kind of bluhh from the plane. *This* tastes good though.
STERLING. Good. I was going to ask your mother whether or not you ate meat but then I completely forgot. I don't, but I'm happy to … [cook it.] *(He's distracted by something up in the tree.)* Look.
BECKY. Where'm I looking?
STERLING. The big tree — one, two, three, four branches from the bottom. See the red on his wing? *(Beat.)* It's a parrot.
BECKY. Shut up! Where? Wait, I can't see! Where? *(Sterling points. Becky moves closer so she can use his arm as a site. Awestruck.)* Oh my God, that's a *parrot*. This is so crazy. You have a *parrot* in your front lawn.
STERLING. *(Amused.)* I know.
BECKY. Oh my God. Do you see them a lot?
STERLING. Only about every two hours. Last week we had a parrot in the kitchen — so I guess, to answer your question, yes, sometimes animals *do* come in the house. Sonia had to chase it out with a … [mop-type-thing.]

BECKY. There are vampire bats here too, right?
STERLING. No, I think those are in Africa, right? If they even exist.
BECKY. I don't know — my friend Tanya came to Costa Rica with her family like two years ago and the maid where they were staying or whatever said if you fall asleep outside after the sun goes down you're supposed to tie a red bandana around your neck or else the vampire bats bite you and suck your blood. *(Sterling smiles.)* I guess bats are scared of red.
STERLING. Aren't they blind?
BECKY. I guess they're mostly blind but they can see red or something?
STERLING. If they're scared of red, why would they drink blood?
BECKY. I don't know! I'm not like, The Nature Master. Oh! I brought you something. Hang on. *(She rifles around in her backpack until she finds a package. Sterling is uneasy. He's not used to chatter.)* They're from my mom. They got a little crushed in my bag, sorry. *(She hands it to him.)*
STERLING. Digestive biscuits! I love digestive biscuits. And these are the best kind — chocolate orange. How exciting! *(He rips into the package and bites into a biscuit. Overjoyed.)* Mmm. *(Chewing.)* Mm-mm. I haven't had a digestive biscuit in years. *(He chews, happily.)* Karen used to have to hide these from me. *(He offers one to Becky. She refuses.)*
BECKY. I didn't have anything to do with what happened to that girl, by the way. *(He chews and listens.)* My mom doesn't believe me — she probly told you that. She says she believes me but I know she doesn't. She thinks I'm lying about like, every little thing. She thinks what everyone else's parents think — that I'm the one that organized the whole party and came up with the idea of inviting Slowgirl and everything. I didn't. I didn't even know there was gonna be a party until like, the very last minute. I mean, it wasn't like it was this big, thought-out thing. Jessie's parents decided *that week* that they were gonna go on a ski trip up at Stratton, I mean, it's not like we sat down a month ago and brainstormed it … and I didn't even know they were gonna invite Slowgirl — her real name's Marybeth, I know it's not a nice nickname but that's what everyone calls her —
STERLING. — Again, Becky, don't feel you have to —
BECKY. — I want to. 'Cause I don't want you thinking the whole time I'm here that I've done something really sick and awful 'cause

I haven't. Plus, I have no idea what my mom told you so you probly think ... whatever, I have no idea what you think. All I did was go to a party just like pretty much every other junior and senior who has friends in the whole entire school. It's so fucked up that I'm pretty much the only one that's like, in trouble.
STERLING. Why does everyone call her Slowgirl?
BECKY. My ex-boyfriend Tyler came up with it. He's such a cocksnot. I don't know, Marybeth's not really, like, retarded? but I mean, something's definitely wrong. I mean, she does math at like a second grade level and her mouth is always kind of half-open, you know? It's not Down syndrome, it's like — I don't know what it is. I think when her mom was pregnant with Marybeth she took some drugs to clear up her skin problem or something, and that's what did it? — that's what everyone says. Anyway, so Jessie was like, "We should totally invite Slowgirl. Wouldn't that be hilarious?" And I know it sounds really mean but seriously?, Slowgirl has no idea when someone's making fun of her. I mean, she's like a golden retriever — I know how awful that sounds, but as long as she's getting attention from someone, she's like, in heaven. *(Beat.)* Why are you making that face?
STERLING. *(Startled.)* What face?
BECKY. Your eyebrows are like, going down.
STERLING. No, sorry ... I'm just listening. *(Pause. Becky's not sure whether she should keep going.)*
BECKY. So when I heard they were gonna invite Slowgirl, I knew how psyched she'd be, so I was like, why not, you know? So Jessie's older brother bought a bunch of vodka and we ended up making Jell-O shots and — none of us knew it or anything but Jell-O's like Slowgirl's favorite food, I mean, she can eat it like 24/7, so we're out on the lawn dancing and everything and we forgot Slowgirl was even at the party. Then someone goes into the kitchen and Slowgirl's in there, wolfing down Jell-O shots, like one after another and we're like, "Marybeth, this isn't just Jell-O. You're only supposed to have two or three." So we hid the rest from her and ... she seemed like she was fine, I mean, she's a big girl, not like, that fat, but her shoulders are like *(Physicalizing it.)* and ... I don't know, she seemed like she was OK. And then I don't really know what happened next 'cause me and Tyler were in Jessie's parents' bedroom the whole time — my parents don't know that part, just so you know. And that's when Marybeth fell out.

STERLING. Fell out?
BECKY. *(Amazed.)* Tch. My mom left that part out? I'm not surprised, actually. Yeah, Marybeth went up to Jessie's dad's office on the second floor and then she climbed out a window and fell onto the concrete by the pool.
STERLING. *(Horrified.)* Is she...?
BECKY. She's pretty bad, I guess. I don't know for sure 'cause they won't tell us. I heard she's in a coma.
STERLING. God.
BECKY. It's so fucked up though — they asked me like a million questions and they didn't ask like, half the other people at the party ... it's like, I'm probly the most outgoing person in my class so I'm friends with pretty much everyone at that party so they assumed I must've organized the whole thing and then, like, pushed her out the window.
STERLING. I'm sure no one thinks that.
BECKY. They do! Why'd I get suspended then?
STERLING. No one else got suspended?
BECKY. Only Jessie. And Tanya for bringing Slowgirl to the party.
STERLING. Well, if they really thought you were responsible, there's no way they'd let you come to Costa Rica ...
BECKY. That's the thing — they didn't. They think I'm like, at home, in my room. They don't need me for any more questioning until next Monday so my mom said as long as I fly back Sunday and just ... don't tell anyone ... *(Pause.)*
STERLING. She didn't mention that. *(Beat.)* Well, I'm sorry, Becky, that's a lot ...
BECKY. Yeah, it sucks. Sucks even more for Marybeth though, I mean, she's the one in a coma. *(Pause.)*
STERLING. So, your boyfriend —
BECKY. — Ex-boyfriend. He dumped me.
STERLING. After // everything ... [happened?]
BECKY. Yeah. His mom wouldn't let him see me anymore so I was like, "Dude, why don't you just sneak out?" I mean, he lives like three streets away, but he said he was too busy with band practice. Then he just stopped calling me. He's basically just a cock and balls — all he does is take Pottery so he can make bongs.
STERLING. How long had you been together?
BECKY. Like five months. Four, I guess. Ugh, I totally hate my life right now.

STERLING. It'll all ... [work out somehow.]
BECKY. So are we, like, in the rainforest?
STERLING. No, this is called a dryforest, though it looks a lot like a rainforest. It still rains a fair amount, especially during the rainy season, but that's not until —
BECKY. — So there must be snakes all over the place.
STERLING. There are some, yes.
BECKY. *(Shuddering.)* Ughh. What, like boa constrictors?
STERLING. No, I've never seen a boa. Mostly garter snakes. Some rattlesnakes. What you really have to watch out for is the coral snakes. They tend to stay down by the river. If you stay on the trails, you should be fine — they tend to clear out when they hear you coming.
BECKY. What do coral snakes look like?
STERLING. Well ... they're red and black and yellow but there are other snakes that look like that — coral snake copycats, I guess, only *they're* not poisonous. I'll show you, I have a laminated guide to the animals of the area. It shows how to tell whether it's a real one. Hector's older brother was killed by a coral snake, actually. You probably shouldn't bring that up with him.
BECKY. For real?
STERLING. Yes. I mean, he probably would've lived if we'd been closer to a hospital but ... if something happens, you have to get to San Jose somehow, probably by helicopter, and even then, Costa Rican medicine is ... [so-so.]
BECKY. Jesus.
STERLING. Yes, so it's best to stay on the trails. *(Beat.)* I don't mean to scare you —
BECKY. — You're not. *(Beat.)* I'm gonna go change if that's cool. I always feel kind of nasty in my travel clothes.
STERLING. Of course. Feel free to take a shower if you want, there's a towel —
BECKY. — No thanks, I just wanna change. *(She goes into the bedroom. Sterling picks up his book and reads a sentence. He puts it down. He watches the parrot. He fishes around in his pocket until he comes up with a pen. He holds the pen an arm's length away, focuses on the tip, and brings it towards his eyes. When it's about two inches away, he stops, holds it there, then does it again. Becky comes out, wearing a tank top. It's skimpier than Sterling's comfortable with.)* Ahh. Much better. *(She takes his smoothie cup and hers and puts them in the kitchen.)*

STERLING. Thanks.
BECKY. Does Sonia do all your dishes?
STERLING. I do most of them.
BECKY. You just leave the really nasty ones for her?
STERLING. That's right. *(Beat.)* So how's your sister?
BECKY. Oh, she's a cunt. You know, she's been at Bowdoin for like eight months so she thinks she like *knows* shit. She basically bitch-slapped me at Christmas for saying "oriental." I was like, "Jesus, Jenna, I slipped and said 'oriental food,' I wasn't like, 'Those kooky orientals.'" Whatever, I'm sure we'll end up being best friends, and she's actually been really cool about what happened. She said I could come live with her if I need to. *(Amused, suddenly.)* When I told her I was gonna visit you she, like ... never mind.
STERLING. What?
BECKY. I shouldn't have started that — sorry. Never mind. *(Pause. Off his look.)* OK, when I told her I was gonna see you, she was like, "You know Uncle Sterling's gay, right?" I was like, "Why do you say that, Jenna?" And she was like, "Come on. Failed marriage, lives alone, talks really softly, into nature." I was like, "Jenna, you just described like *ev*-ery psycho-killah." *(Catching herself.)* No offense or anything.
STERLING. No ...
BECKY. I wasn't like, hoping you weren't gay — I don't care.
STERLING. That's funny that she thinks that. *(Beat.)* I'm not, by the way —
BECKY. — Oh, I wasn't asking you to like // clarify it —
STERLING. No, I know. I don't know why I felt the need to ...
BECKY. I didn't think you were. I'm not either. Tanya and I felt each other up at a party once but neither of us, like, got off on it. It was kind of a joke. What's with the eye thing?
STERLING. Sorry?
BECKY. With the pen and everything?
STERLING. Oh, I have, um ... they call it a "convergence insufficiency." Basically, my pupils can't agree on a fixed point up to about two feet from my face.
BECKY. *(Concerned.)* That sucks. So what, you can't see?
STERLING. Oh no — it's nothing really, I just get headaches when I read. I've got special glasses with prisms in them so that helps, but —
BECKY. *(Amused.)* — Prisms?? Like, pyramids?

STERLING. No — they're these. *(The glasses he's wearing. Becky takes them off his face and tries them on. They're strong. Sterling would like them back.)* They help, but supposedly if you can build up your eye muscles, your eyes won't have as much trouble turning in towards each other when you read, so your headaches won't be so bad. I try and do the pen exercise about five times a day. *(Becky gives them back.)*
BECKY. That's so geeky.
STERLING. I know.
BECKY. Were you like, a geek in high school? *(He's not sure whether she's razzing him or she actually wants an answer.)* Did you wear a fanny pack?
STERLING. No.
BECKY. Did they even have fanny packs back then?
STERLING. *(Mock offended.)* Yes.
BECKY. You *know* because you had one in like *ev*-ery color. *(Beat.)* So you don't … do you have a girlfriend or anything?
STERLING. No.
BECKY. How long has it been since you had a girlfriend?
STERLING. Well, Karen was seven years ago.
BECKY. She was the last one?
STERLING. Yes.
BECKY. Are you guys still in touch?
STERLING. No, no.
BECKY. How long were you married?
STERLING. Six years.
BECKY. *(Amazed.)* Whoa. And then you moved here right after that?
STERLING. No, I traveled on the West Coast for a while, sort of … around where she was. Then I knew I wanted to live abroad but I didn't know where, so … someone said there was still cheap land in Costa Rica so I came down here and … liked it. *(She applies some Chapstick.)*
BECKY. Want some?
STERLING. No thanks.
BECKY. Do you miss being in America?
STERLING. In the States? Sometimes.
BECKY. *(Thinking.)* Yeah, I'd probly blow my brains out if I were here by myself — no offense or anything, it's really beautiful but, I'm too much of a people person. Even last week when I was suspended, I started going out of my mind. That's probly why my mom said I should get out of the house. I mean, I was getting *crazy*

— I was like, freaking myself out. Do you mind if I make a tiny bit more smoothie?
STERLING. Help yourself. The fruit's in the freezer —
BECKY. — I know, in the handy little freezer baggies — it's so cute. Do you want a little more?
STERLING. Sure. Please. *(She scampers into the kitchen and starts making the smoothies.)* How do you mean you were "getting crazy"?
BECKY. Oh, not like crazy-crazy but like ... you're gonna think I'm such a freak but I have this Neutrogena acne cleanser? It's like this white stuff and you put it on your face and then let it dry? Well, last week I put it on and then looked at myself in the mirror and I looked *just* like a dead clown so I started making these dead clown faces at myself and then I started laughing hysterically and I couldn't stop. I think I was in the bathroom for like an hour and a half, just laughing my head off. It really freaked my mom out. *(She blends the smoothies.)* Now you probly think I'm like a total psycho-killah.
STERLING. No ...
BECKY. Do you even have a phone here?
STERLING. I have one of those —
BECKY. — I don't need one, I was just wondering —
STERLING. *(He WILL get this sentence out.)* — I have one of those international cell phones. You're welcome to use it whenever you want, the only thing is, it really only works if you go up to the top of the hill, by the labyrinth.
BECKY. The labyrinth?
STERLING. Yes.
BECKY. What's that?
STERLING. I'll take you up there tomorrow ... Hector and I built a walking labyrinth based on the one at Chartres, near Paris.
BECKY. I have no idea what that is.
STERLING. Oh ... it's a cathedral. When you walk in, there's this maze-type thing — the monks used to walk around — we'll go up there. You kind of have to see it.
BECKY. *Salute.*
STERLING. *Salud.* It's wonderful to see you. I'm sorry I've been a bit of an absentee uncle ... I know I should be keeping better tabs on you but it's tough with your dad ...
BECKY. Yeah, my dad really didn't want me to come down here. I

mean, first off, he didn't want me to leave when I wasn't supposed to, but then when my mom said she'd bought a ticket for me to visit you, he basically flipped.
STERLING. I imagine.
BECKY. He and my mom got in a gigundous fight about it — they're probably divorced by now. Did you and my dad always hate each other?
STERLING. No, no. We always liked each other, actually — we used to play chess. It was all a big misunderstanding. It's too bad 'cause it keeps me from seeing much of you and Jenna and your mother. Your mother and I were best friends when we were growing up.
BECKY. Yeah, that's what she says. She said you had "Book Club," just the two of you.
STERLING. *(Amused.)* Yes. *(Beat.)* Well, you must be exhausted, I'll let you —
BECKY. — Not really. I think I drank too much smoothie though. I feel bloated. *(Putting a hand on her stomach to feel what's going on in there.)* Ugh, I totally hate my life right now.
STERLING. I think it's good that you're getting away. People always feel better when they get into the sunshine — all the Vitamin D. I always say that and it always sounds so stupid. I think your grandmother used to say that, "Vitamin D." Anyway, I'll take you into town later. There's really nothing to see except a bunch of tin boxes and a church and a pool table and some roosters running around in the road.
BECKY. That sounds awesome. Actually, maybe I'll take a nap in the hammock first? Just for a few minutes. *(She fishes her trendy music gadget and earphones out of her backpack.)*
STERLING. Sure. It takes some getting used to. I capsized for the first year. *(Becky laughs. She gets into the hammock no problem.)* Wow, you're a natural. Sweet dreams. *(Becky puts in her earphones. She closes her eyes and swings herself with her foot. Sterling watches her. He can hear her music, barely. He is uneasy. Sound of a howler monkey off in the distance. Lights fade.)*

Scene 2

Tuesday afternoon. The labyrinth.

The labyrinth consists of ankle-high stones arranged in eleven concentric circles. Becky sits on a tree stump in the center, chewing gum and watching Sterling walk. There are wooden crosses just beyond the labyrinth's outermost circle. Sterling's hands are clasped together in front of him like a monk's. Every once in a while, his lips move. Becky finds this disturbing.

BECKY. Are you like, praying?
STERLING. I usually walk in silence.
BECKY. Sorry. *(Beat.)* So I'm not allowed to talk *at all*? *(No response.)* I'm just trying to figure out how to do it — so you like, walk and pray at the same time?
STERLING. I'm not praying.
BECKY. What were you just saying then?
STERLING. Nothing.
BECKY. Come on, I saw your lips moving. *(Sterling smiles.)* How about I get to talk 'cause I'm not doing it but you have to be quiet 'cause you are? *(He keeps walking.)* Yeah, I like that … OK, what're we gonna talk about? — I mean, what am *I* gonna talk about? Hmm … that coffee you made me is like *(Singing it.)* crack-cocaine. Oh! — I saw an anteater this morning when I went for a walk. I'm almost positive. *(She gets off the stump and adjusts an out-of-place stone. Sterling is obviously agitated by this.)* I'm gonna call him Blondie. He was *so* cute — I would totally go out with him, like, *to*-night. Can you imagine, like … *(Delicately frenching an anteater.)* He'd probly be a *way* better kisser than Tyler — Tyler was like HAVE YOU MET MY TONGUE? I'm like [grossed out.] Yeah, we met. Blondie didn't even care that I was like stalking him, he was just like, do-di-do *(Physicalizing puttering along.)* I was like *(Slight Latina accent.)* "Stop on by, dawg, you know where I live — I'm in *the* house." *(Meaning the only house in sight.)*
STERLING. Do you mind! [not fucking with my stone.]

BECKY. *(Taken aback.)* What? I was // fixing it.
STERLING. I try to … thank you but I try to walk the labyrinth as it is, then afterward, if a stone's out of place, I fix it.
BECKY. *(Stung.)* Sorry. I didn't get the manual.
STERLING. No … [don't worry about it.] *(He wishes he hadn't said anything. Pause.)*
BECKY. God, I didn't know you were such a hardcore Christian.
STERLING. I'm not.
BECKY. Then what's with the crosses?
STERLING. People from the village brought them up.
BECKY. Ew, creepy — they just like … *(Gesture: satanically sticking them the ground.)*
STERLING. Every Easter they do the fourteen stations of the cross all the way up the trail and then everyone walks the labyrinth together. *(Pointedly.)* In silence. I just haven't taken the crosses down yet. *(Pause.)*
BECKY. My mom thinks you're a Buddhist, you know. But she said she's not really sure these days.
STERLING. I did study Buddhism.
BECKY. Can you levitate?
STERLING. No. *(Beat.)* I was very into Shinto for a while.
BECKY. What's that?
STERLING. It's a Japanese belief system. I was studying it when Hector and I were building this labyrinth, actually. *(Becky picks at a speck of dirt on her t-shirt. She lifts it slightly to check if the inside is dirty too. Sterling notices, and then makes a point of not looking at her.)*
BECKY. Is it like Buddhism?
STERLING. Yes, sort of. They believe there's a god in everything around us — every tree, every rock, every leaf —
BECKY. *(Hopping up.)* — OK, I wanna try. Do I have to start at the outside and go in, or can I do it the other way?
STERLING. However you want. I usually start from the outside.
BECKY. OK, I'll start on the inside and go out so we can crash into each other in the middle.
STERLING. Alright. Let's try and do it in silence. *(Becky mouths "OK." They start walking.)*
BECKY. You're not gonna start over? *(Reluctantly, he does. They walk for a few steps.)*
BECKY. I feel like I'm worshipping Satan.
STERLING. Alright, let's talk our way through this one. Tomor-

row we'll do it —
BECKY. — Fine. *(Beat.)* Am I supposed to be thinking about God or something?
STERLING. You can think about whatever you want to.
BECKY. What's it supposed to do?
STERLING. What do you mean?
BECKY. What's the point?
STERLING. I don't know. Maybe just see how it hits you. The point used to be either pilgrimage or repentance. If you were doing it as a pilgrimage, they'd call it the "Road to Jerusalem" because you were substituting it for … you know, the actual trip. If you were doing it for repentance, you were supposed to do it on your knees. I don't recommend that. *(Beat.)* I like doing it because it calms me down — straightens out my head. It's different for everyone, I imagine.
BECKY. Are you supposed to like, breathe at the same time as you step — I mean, are they supposed to be like … *(A couple exaggerated breaths/steps, like a clunky robot.)*
STERLING. You can't do it wrong, Becky. Just do it however you want.
BECKY. OK. I'm not gonna think about God then 'cause I don't believe in God.
STERLING. No?
BECKY. No. I stopped believing in God — I know the exact moment too. I was watching TV and this tornado, like, wiped out this whole entire town in Missouri, I think? I mean their middle school — it was like someone picked it up and *chucked* it. And they were interviewing all these religious guys from all over the place and asking them how they explain the fact that God trashed this entire town and every answer was like such a load of shit, I mean, some of them were like, "God didn't do it — he doesn't have power over *every* thing, only *some* things," and I was like, Dude, are you hearing yourself through your earpiece?? But … so *you* do?
STERLING. Believe in God?
BECKY. Yeah.
STERLING. Yes.
BECKY. What, like the Christian God?
STERLING. Not exactly.
BECKY. What God then?
STERLING. My own, I guess.
BECKY. So does your own God, like, chuck people's middle

schools then?
STERLING. I don't know.
BECKY. Yeah, but what do you think?
STERLING. I don't know. I don't think about it quite in those terms ... *(Becky sighs loudly. He's being difficult.)*
BECKY. Doesn't this make you dizzy?
STERLING. No.
BECKY. I'm getting dizzy.
STERLING. Shoot! I should've brought some water up. I forgot to tell you — you've got to drink about three times as much as you're used to. *(Beat.)* Becky, it's on my mind so I have to bring it up ... the rum ...
BECKY. *(Dumbfounded.)* What, do you like, measure it every day?
STERLING. No ... it's not a big deal, I'd just ... I'd rather I knew when you were having a drink —
BECKY. *(Fiery.)* — Fine, I had one drink last night at 10:37 P.M. Rum and soda.
STERLING. OK, you don't have to get upset ... I could care less if you have a drink every once in a while, I just want to make sure you're not —
BECKY. — I'm not gonna like, go on a binge at my uncle's casa.
STERLING. I know that.
BECKY. I thought the point was for me to relax here.
STERLING. It is.
BECKY. Don't normal people relax with a drink?
STERLING. Yes.
BECKY. Then why are you getting on my case?
STERLING. I'm not getting on your case, I just ... *(Long uncomfortable silence. They walk.)*
BECKY. So how was that blowjob from Sonia this morning? *(Sterling stops walking.)* It looked like fun. I mean, I didn't watch or anything — that'd be nasty. I went out for a walk but then I realized I forgot to put sunscreen on the tips of my ears — I always forget that — so I came back and wah-bam!, you guys don't waste any time.
STERLING. *(Mortified.)* I'm sorry you saw that.
BECKY. Whatever, I don't care. I mean, you're a guy, you're out in the middle of nowhere, there's one woman around, she's hot, she works for you —

STERLING. — That's not —
BECKY. — Whatever, I don't care! It's not like I'm gonna go spread it around town. Go *tell Los Angeles.* So are you guys, like, in love?
STERLING. No.
BECKY. Is she in love with you?
STERLING. No, I don't think so.
BECKY. You should be careful, Sterling. Women fall in love like sixty percent faster than guys — I read that when me and my mom were in line at the grocery store and this geriatric guy in front of us was buying like ninety vegetables. It has to do with hormones, I think. Women are just like, hooked up for it. *(Beat.)* I was never really into blowjobs when I was going out with Tyler but maybe that's 'cause he wanted one like every two hours.
STERLING. *(Wildly uncomfortable.)* Becky, I can't continue this conversation.
BECKY. Sorry, jeeze. I told you, I'm like the most outgoing person in my school — stuff comes into my head and I just say it, you know? I don't like, check where it fits in on the "appropriate topics" scale or whatever. Jesus Christ, I don't see what the big deal is — it's just a blowjob. Oops, I'm probly not supposed to say "Jesus Christ" while I'm in here, am I? *(Nothing from Sterling. He starts walking again.)*
BECKY. So, just so I know, does Hector know about it?
STERLING. Of course not.
BECKY. How long has it been going on?
STERLING. A while — it's nothing. Anyway. *(They walk in silence.)*
BECKY. Oooommmmmm. *(Nothing from Sterling. They keep walking.)* Ooooooooooommmmmmmmmmmmmmmm. *(Beat.)* OK, I just felt it.
STERLING. What?
BECKY. *(Sincere.)* I felt, um … spiritual. *(Sterling laughs.)* What? Don't laugh — I'm serious. I felt it for a second. It was like a deep, inner calm or something — just for a second.
STERLING. That's good. You should come up by yourself tomorrow. That's when you get the full effect.
BECKY. I think that'd freak me out. Let's do silent day tomorrow and then I'll come up by myself on Thursday.
STERLING. Fine.
BECKY. Shit, Friday's my dad's birthday — you *have to* remind me to call him. I probly should've called my folks to tell them I got

here OK.
STERLING. There hasn't been any cell signal. It goes in and out.
BECKY. Good, I'll tell them that. *(Beat.)* I still don't get why my dad doesn't like you.
STERLING. Have you asked him?
BECKY. Yeah, he won't say. I think my mom told him not to.
STERLING. Your dad thinks I'm a crook.
BECKY. Are you?
STERLING. No.
BECKY. It's OK if you are.
STERLING. Thank you, but I'm not.
BECKY. So why does he think that then?
STERLING. Because my former partner is a crook. Brett. He's in prison now.
BECKY. Why?
STERLING. He ... we were best friends in law school and we started our own practice after we graduated. We represented severely ... disadvantaged people, most of whom had been victims of ... well, various awful situations. *(Better stop here.)*.
BECKY. Yeah? ...
STERLING. I'm not sure what your folks would want you to know.
BECKY. *(Screw that.)* What do *you* want me to know?
STERLING. Well ... there was a whole complicated ordeal but basically what happened is, money that should've been compensation for fifty-five people ended up in an account called "James Maxwell" ... which is the name of a man who doesn't exist, though according to our records, he was a consultant of ours. A very well-paid consultant.
BECKY. Whoa.
STERLING. It went on for years — I had no idea. Eventually, when we were audited and they found the account, it turned into a huge story because four of the people who didn't get their compensation were Holocaust survivors. Brett was sentenced to fifteen years, I was acquitted. *(Pause.)*
BECKY. So then you just came down here?
STERLING. Then Karen left me. She didn't believe I ... well, she thought what your dad thought: that I was a crook. So ... *(Choosing his words carefully.)* then I followed her around California for about two years, and when that didn't pan out, I went through a kind of black hole and then came down here.

BECKY. Did the Holocaust survivors end up getting their money?
STERLING. Oh — they sued us — they got their money times five.
BECKY. Are you still in touch with Brett?
STERLING. No. Someone forwarded me a letter from him a while back but I didn't respond. It was more or less an apology.
BECKY. And you never hear from Karen?
STERLING. No. She doesn't know I'm down here. Anyway, building this labyrinth was probably the best thing I've ever done. I walk it at night when there's a full moon — you can do it without flashlights or anything.
BECKY. Whoa, that's cool. I should make one in our back lawn. We'd probly have Massachusetts' only walking labyrinth. *(Beat.)* You can definitely feel a ... I don't know.
STERLING. A what?
BECKY. Like ... a purpose or something, like it's meant to be here. It feels ... solid. *(Beat.)* I don't know what the best thing I've ever done is — I haven't really done anything that good yet. I wrote a book of poems when I was a freshman.
STERLING. Really?
BECKY. Yeah. I spent a really long time on them. They're bad. I'm still proud of them though, I guess. I like the idea anyway. I took one minute and wrote down the names of everyone in my head — friends, family, characters on TV, people who are dead, lead singers from bands, guys I've fucked, everyone, and then I wrote a poem about each one — everyone who was in my head in that one minute. Twenty-eight poems.
STERLING. That's a fantastic idea.
BECKY. You and Karen had a poem in there but it was one of the *really* bad ones — sorry. I thought about giving it to you this week but ... no. It's got oysters in it or something stupid.
STERLING. I'm flattered. Have you kept up with your poetry?
BECKY. No. I still want to be a poet but that's stupid, I mean, who's actually a poet?
STERLING. Robert Frost, Emily Dickenson —
BECKY. — No, I mean like, right now. Who's actually making a living as a poet right now?
STERLING. There are ways. You can get grants and teach ... there are ways to do everything.
BECKY. Whatever, I'll have plenty of time to write poetry if I go

to prison.
STERLING. What are you talking about?
BECKY. I might go to prison. That's what they told me.
STERLING. Who told you that?
BECKY. Everybody — the principal, the police, pretty much everybody. They gave me this printout of a case in Colorado where this girl who's seventeen like me went to prison for doing the exact same thing they think I did. Basically just being in the wrong place. They're just waiting to see what happens to Marybeth. *(This hits Sterling hard. He looks like he's going to pass out.)*
BECKY. What's wrong?
STERLING. Nothing.
BECKY. Are you alright?
STERLING. I'll sit …
BECKY. *(Alarmed.)* What's wrong?
STERLING. I should've brought some water up …
BECKY. Want me to run and get some?
STERLING. No, I'll be fine … just … *(He sits down and takes some deep breaths. Becky watches him. She feels his forehead. He flinches.)*
STERLING. I don't understand why you're in worse trouble than everyone else.
BECKY. 'Cause they know I was in the room when they were doing the wings.
STERLING. The wings?
BECKY. Yeah, Marybeth had this — after she did all those Jell-O shots, she went around telling everyone how she felt like she was flying and … this was so stupid — I had nothing to do with this — so, Jessie's brother found this kite in the basement and they got some scissors and cut the kite in half and then duct-taped them to Marybeth's arms and — it sounds really awful, but it wasn't — I mean, she was having the time of her life. She was running around the dining room table, flapping away, going, "I'm a bird, I'm a plane, I'm Marybeth Holliman," I mean, seriously — I don't think I've ever seen anyone so happy in my life. And then we kind of … Tyler and I went into the bedroom and everyone did their own thing or went outside to dance or whatever and I guess Marybeth like, got up on the window ledge and … tried to fly or something. The thing is, I'm in more trouble than everyone else 'cause they think I was like, actually there when she got up on the ledge and stuff, which I wasn't — I was in the bedroom with Tyler the whole time.

STERLING. Is Tyler in trouble too?
BECKY. No. He told the police he went home before everything happened and then he got his parents and his neighbors to say they all saw him at home watching TV, which is like, total bullshit 'cause we were having sex the whole time everything was going on. No one else will even say they saw Tyler at the party 'cause his dad's like this superstar lawyer and everyone's afraid of him.
STERLING. Does your mother believe you weren't in the room?
BECKY. No. She says she does but ... I never know what my mom thinks. She just thinks whatever my dad thinks.
STERLING. What does your dad think?
BECKY. He says he believes me but ... I don't know, he's so depressed about it he basically doesn't come home from work anymore.
STERLING. So who else is in trouble?
BECKY. I told you: Jessie for having the party, her brother for buying the vodka, Tanya for bringing Slowgirl, and me.
STERLING. That's it.
BECKY. Pretty much, yeah.
STERLING. Do you have a lawyer?
BECKY. Yeah, my dad found some guy who went to Harvard or whatever — he smells really weird ... like when you open a plastic toy and it's that really plasticky smell? That's what he smells like. Whatever, he's probly really smart. Ugh, I should just never go home. Why can't I just stay here, Sterling? Please don't make me go home.
STERLING. You're welcome here whenever you like.
BECKY. Why don't I just stay here and we'll tell the people in the village we're married — wouldn't that be hilarious? Just to see what they say. We'll tell them I'm your trophy wife. *(He won't play along with this one.)*
BECKY. We should smoke a bowl together. *(Beat.)* You probly grow here, right? Come on ... you can tell me.
STERLING. No, I don't.
BECKY. I'm sure Hector does.
STERLING. I don't know.
BECKY. Oh, you guys probly smoke up like twice a day. I would, if I lived here. Whatever, you don't have to tell me. *(Long pause.)* What's really screwing me over now is, some of it's on tape.
STERLING. What is?
BECKY. Marybeth falling and all that. It's on tape. Jessie was like,

29

"*No* pictures, *no* video," but her brother's friend had this old-school video camera? — He said it didn't even work but it did and … whatever, it ended up with the police. He was like, filming goofy stuff like people dancing and dry humping each other — I don't know, I didn't see it — but I guess then the camera goes up and you see Marybeth way up in the window and she flaps her wings a few times and then she just falls. *(Exasperated.)* I mean, it's crazy 'cause the swimming pool's literally touching the side of the house, I mean, Jessie's dad had it built that way so they could see inside the pool from a window in the basement and, I mean, they never ended up doing the window 'cause they were afraid the glass would break and it would flood the house but still, the pool's like *right* there, I mean, if you or I stepped out of the window, we'd have to like *try* not to land in the deep end. It just — it makes no sense whatsoever. It's like she was trying to hit the concrete.
STERLING. Are you in the video?
BECKY. See that's the thing — Tanya told me that right before Slowgirl got up on the ledge, you can see me up in the window like, laughing and adjusting her wing but she said you can basically only see my arm and that's *so* fucked up 'cause I wasn't even there. I was definitely like, helping her attach the wing earlier for like a few seconds but that was at least a half-hour before. So either it's someone else's arm or someone fucked with the tape. *(Sterling's quiet.)* You don't believe me, do you?
STERLING. I'm just listening.
BECKY. That's exactly what my mom would've said.
STERLING. I —
BECKY. — You couldn't come right out and say, "No, I don't believe you, Becky" so you had to say the same thing in, like, an underhanded way.
STERLING. That's your interpretation // of what I said.
BECKY. See, my mom would've said that too. But it's not *my* interpretation. It's *the* interpretation of someone // saying that.
STERLING. Well, that's wrong because it's not true that I don't believe you.
BECKY. So you *do* believe me?
STERLING. I … *(Beat.)* I know *that* makes it sound like the answer is "no" but try and understand this, Becky. I'm not interested in being a judge or … detective or … I'm your godfather and your uncle so —

BECKY. — So that means you — [automatically believe me?]
STERLING. — Let me finish, for a sec. I'm your godfather and uncle so ... I just need to *(Getting choked up.)* ... I'm sorry — I'm not good at this ... *(He's having trouble talking. She can barely watch him say this.)* I'm trying to help you but I ... I'm sorry I haven't visited you enough and I ... I got very worried when you had a drink without telling me ... I worry — that's *my* problem ... that's why I'm not very good at being around people because I don't ... know what to say ... I say the wrong thing and I ... try to ... I'm sorry. Do you understand at all?
BECKY. Yes.
STERLING. I want to help you.
BECKY. Thank you.
STERLING. Yes, I believe you. Yes. I always believe you.
BECKY. Thanks. *(Long pause. She takes out her Chapstick and holds it two feet from her face, then brings it in towards her eyes.)* Do I stop now?
STERLING. You stop when you start to see two images.
BECKY. *(Moving it a little closer.)* Right here. Now what?
STERLING. That's it. Then you do it again.
BECKY. The exact same way?
STERLING. Yes.
BECKY. Huh. *(Lights fade.)*

Scene 3

Thursday night. Sterling's house.

It's the middle of the night. Darkness. Becky and Sterling have gone to sleep. She's on the fold-out and he's in his bedroom. Because of the gap between the bedroom wall and the ceiling, they can hear each other well. A loud scurrying/scratching sound.

BECKY. *(Sitting up.)* What the f...? *(It stops.)* Ugh. *(It starts up again.)* Dude! *(Beat.)* Hey!
STERLING. *(Sleepily.)* It's OK. It's an iguana.

BECKY. *(Sharply.)* How's that "OK"?
STERLING. It's just their toenails on the tin ... they like to go up there at night.
BECKY. Well, tell 'em to get the fuck down. Tell Sonia to get 'em down. *(Beat.)* Or is that not in her job description?
STERLING. Easy.
BECKY. I'm not playin' — isn't the iguana in the dragon family? *(Nothing from him.)* Yes, it is. *(Beat.)* Can't they just come down off the roof and like ... come in?
STERLING. They don't.
BECKY. How do you know? Maybe they come in when you're sleeping.
STERLING. Maybe.
BECKY. Ugh. No fair — you have a door. *(Scurrying sound, quieter this time.)* Dude!! They're like sharpening their claws on your roof — oh my God, Sterling, your house is like a horror movie from the '80s. *(Beat.)* My mom's gonna be *pissed* at you if an iguana rapes me. *(Sterling chuckles.)* Seriously, how do you sleep in here?
STERLING. They didn't bother you for the last three nights.
BECKY. I haven't even *been* here three nights.
STERLING. Um ... it's Thursday // and you ... [got here Monday.]
BECKY. Whoa! — You *have to* remind me to call my dad tomorrow. *(Beat.)* Well whatever, they weren't up there the last three nights.
STERLING. They're up there every night, except in the rainy season.
BECKY. *(Snapping.)* No they weren't. *(Pause.)*
STERLING. Do you want to switch? I'm happy to take the fold-out ...
BECKY. No. You need your beauty sleep.
STERLING. Thank you. Goodnight, Becky.
BECKY. Goodnight, Sterling. *(Beat.)* I hope a dragon doesn't like rip into your torso and lay its eggs in you.
STERLING. Thank you.
BECKY. It won't, obviously, 'cause you have a door.
STERLING. Lucky me. Goodnight.
BECKY. Goodnight. *(Beat.)* I'm not even tired // anymore.
STERLING. *(To himself, annoyed.)* Oh my God. *(Louder.)* You're welcome to read or ... the light won't keep me up — I sleep through anything.

BECKY. Duh. *(Beat.)* Do you have any Xanax?
STERLING. No.
BECKY. Ambien?
STERLING. No. I have chamomile.
BECKY. Ugh, are you my gramma? *(She sighs loudly. Then she starts giggling.)*
STERLING. What?
BECKY. I feel like we're having a sleepover. We should have matching PJ's. Are you wearing PJ's in there?
STERLING. No.
BECKY. *(Quietly.)* Ew. *(Beat.)*
STERLING. *(Chuckling.)* Your mom and I used to have matching PJ's.
BECKY. Ohh! … that's so cute. Did they have like, duckies on them?
STERLING. They were plaid.
BECKY. Ohhh … Did they have feeties?
STERLING. Feedies?
BECKY. *(Get with it.)* Feet.
STERLING. Oh … yes.
BECKY. Ohhhh.
STERLING. Anyway. Sweet dreams.
BECKY. You too. *(Pause.)* Hey, Sterling?
STERLING. *(Slightly annoyed.)* Yes?
BECKY. Do you think you're gonna die down here? *(Pause. He sounds more awake from now on.)*
STERLING. Yes, probably.
BECKY. You wanna be buried in the labyrinth, right?
STERLING. No … I'll probably — [get cremated.]
BECKY. — OH, duh, you wanna get cremated. That's what all you hippies want — so you don't "take up space"?
STERLING. That's right.
BECKY. Mm. I wanna die outside. I don't wanna die in like a hospital or a geriatric home — that's grim. I wanna make sure if my soul gets released at the exact moment I die, it goes right back into nature and not into like, cheesy wallpaper.
STERLING. That makes sense.
BECKY. I know. *(Beat.)* I don't understand those people who want, like, gigundous temples built for them when they die, you know? It's like, who *are* you? *(The bedroom door swings open suddenly and Sterling steps out. He's in sweatpants and a T-shirt. Becky's startled.)*

BECKY. Oh whoa, hey.
STERLING. Sorry … just need some water. *(He turns on the kitchen light. He fills up his mug from the water carton by the sink. It's almost empty.)* Can I get you some?
BECKY. No thanks. *(She watches him. She's fascinated by how methodically he does everything.)*
STERLING. Hector needs to get us another. *(He turns off the light and heads back to the bedroom.)*
BECKY. Actually, yeah, I'll have some — sorry. *(He nods and fills up a mug for her. He brings it over.)* Thanks. *(She takes a sip.)* Hey, can I ask you something?
STERLING. Sure.
BECKY. Sorry — are you like, exhausted?
STERLING. No, what's up? *(She turns on her reading light.)*
BECKY. What'd you mean by "black hole"?
STERLING. *(As though he doesn't remember.)* Um …
BECKY. You know, when you said you went through a black hole before you came down here — what'd you mean?
STERLING. Well … I'd lost Karen and I had a lot to figure out. Everything, really. I had to … start over.
BECKY. So were you like, wicked depressed?
STERLING. *(Sitting.)* I was, yes.
BECKY. Mm.
STERLING. And scared.
BECKY. Of what?
STERLING. Everything. What was happening, I told you, with Brett and —
BECKY. *(Quickly.)* — But you didn't know about that, right?
STERLING. I didn't.
BECKY. But so the vacation money, is that what you were mainly — ? *(Sterling just looks at her. Oops … did she put her foot in it?)* I mean, is that why you were scared?
STERLING. *(Coolly.)* I don't remember telling you about that.
BECKY. Oh, my mom just said — I was asking her stuff before I came down here and — she didn't say much but she said when you were visiting us, right before you went to England, you told her you were worried about all the vacation money Brett was giving you or something?
STERLING. Mm. *(Had his sister told her everything?)* Brett didn't *give* me the money, it was my salary. We just … we seemed to sud-

34

denly be making an awful lot and ... it seemed to magically cover our vacations and anything we wanted and ... Karen was enjoying that immensely ... I just didn't quite understand where that money was coming from. *(Beat.)* Is that more or less what your mom told you?
BECKY. But you guys were lawyers. Don't lawyers make *bank?*
STERLING. Not our kind of lawyers.
BECKY. So wait, the England trip was years before the whole James Maxwell thing.
STERLING. Right.
BECKY. So this vacation money you were worried about is *not* the money he's in prison for.
STERLING. Right.
BECKY. I'm just trying to understand.
STERLING. I know.
BECKY. So, you're saying Brett was like ... totally shady the whole time you were working together.
STERLING. *(Slightly defensive.)* I don't know that.
BECKY. Were you ever like, "Hey Brett, where's all this money comin' from?"
STERLING. Good question. No. We'd been working together since ... well, I told you, since graduation, and ... this is my failure but — I've never paid attention to money ... I haven't balanced a checkbook since I was twenty, so —
BECKY. — Didn't you think it might've been a good time // to start?
STERLING. Brett was the numbers guy — I liked not having to worry about that. I could just work and travel and ... be with Karen, who needed a certain level of ... flurry. Money depresses me.
BECKY. But so they investigated all the paperwork and everything?
STERLING. Yes.
BECKY. All the way back? Or just James Maxwell? *(He smiles. She'd make an excellent lawyer.)*
STERLING. Mostly James Maxwell. They tried to go all the way back but ... Brett was pretty clever and ... most of it had been spent by then. So yes, I'm sure I could've been more helpful to them but ... *(Listening for the iguanas overhead.)* we all just ... survive. *(Pause.)*
BECKY. Wait. Are you like, *in hiding* in South America?
STERLING. No ... it's my home. "Central." I just don't feel particularly welcome in the States anymore.
BECKY. *(Excited.)* You mean like ... by the Feds?

35

STERLING. *(Amused.)* No.
BECKY. You mean Karen?
STERLING. I just like it here. Anyway ...
BECKY. Why don't you come back and hang out with us, just for a little bit? — Oh! Why don't you come back for my mom's Save-the-Library party? — it's like sinking or something *(Who cares?)* — you could *totally* geek-out with her! You wouldn't have to stay with us — you could stay at the Marriott — they have the *nastiest* breakfast buffet but they have *huge* tubs — Tanya's parents got us a room after Winter Ball — we tried to get a picture with like, *everyone* in the tub *(Most hilarious night ever.)* Ooohh ... we could surprise my mom! — I'll be in prison but — oh my god, she would *flip*. Do it!
STERLING. *(No way.)* Uh ...
BECKY. You could be my lawyer.
STERLING. I'm not that kind of lawyer.
BECKY. *(Rejected.)* I know, duh. *(Pause.)*
STERLING. I wish I could be there for your mom's party and everything else, Becky, but ... I'm here now. *(Faint scratching sound again. Becky looks up, nervously.)*
STERLING. Do you usually sleep pretty well at home?
BECKY. Usually, yeah — Jenna's the insomniac. *(Beat.)* I don't sleep that well these days.
STERLING. Did you uh ... did you want to try and get to sleep?
BECKY. I'm not tired. You? *(Sterling shakes his head.)*
STERLING. I wanted to ask you ... ... how you're doing.
BECKY. In what sense?
STERLING. In any sense, just ... you're going through so much and ... it's a lot of fun having you here and, I know you're wanting to get away from it ... I just wanted to know how you're doing.
BECKY. I'm OK. I woke up this morning and I was just like ... fahhk, you know? like, random moments from the party keep playing over and over in my head and I can't stop them. Like cars honking and ... *(Thinking.)* Right when we came in and Slowgirl had been eating those Jell-O shots? she had this little triangle of orange Jell-O on her chin and I was like, "Hold on, Marybeth, let's get a napkin," and I started to wipe her face but she *(The scratching/scurrying again.)* — Jesus! that's fucking creepy *(She listens ... it stops.)* ... so Marybeth wanted to do it herself so she like wiped *every* part of her face except for where the Jell-O chunk was, and it

36

was *hil*-arious and I started laughing, and then she started laughing and then she *totally* turned it into a comedy routine — she was like wiping the napkin all over her body like she was trying to find the Jell-O chunk ... we were laughing our asses off. *(Beat.)* I don't know though, when I think about going back home and answering more questions from the police and sitting there at dinner while my dad's trying as hard as he can not to look at me — it kind of makes me feel like, what's the point, you know? But ... *(Hoping he'll have a magical answer. Long pause. He doesn't.)* You wanna know what I thought of, though? When I was on my walk today? I was thinking this is the lowest point I've ever been, both like, on the globe and ... in my life. Isn't that weird?
STERLING. It is. It's funny how sometimes those things — *(Sudden, loud, frantic scurrying. Becky looks genuinely terrified. Her body contracts into a protective position. She buries her face in her bedding and shrieks. It's as though the world is scratching its way down onto her. Sterling needs to do something NOW.)* It's OK! It's OK ... they're just moving around up there. Hold on, I'll ... *(He grabs a broom from the bathroom. He bashes the ceiling five times with the butt.)*
BECKY. Stop it!! *(Pause.)*
STERLING. You take the bedroom. I'll sleep here. *(She gathers her bedding. He leans the broom against the wall. She looks so young, disoriented. How'd she get here? She wanders into the bedroom and closes the door.)* If you put the fan on, it drowns out the noise. *(Nothing from her. The bedroom goes dark. Sterling sits down on the fold-out, waiting for the iguanas to start up again. He gets up and grabs the broom. He sits back down. He's in over his head. Lights fade.)*

Scene 4

Saturday night. Sterling's house.

Sterling is sitting out on the steps. There are two place settings beside him. He looks around, concerned. He takes a pebble out of his pocket and places it next to Becky's plate. He picks up his fork and brings it in towards his eyes, slowly. He does it again. In walks Becky, out of breath, swinging a fistful of tropical foliage. There's something strange about her — she's giggly and her words are coming out funny.

STERLING. Hey.
BECKY. Hey.
STERLING. That was a long walk.
BECKY. Yeah, I did the labyrinth *twice* and then I did the lower, lower trail. *(She starts giggling.)*
STERLING. What? [is so funny?]
BECKY. *(Imitating him.)* What? *(She giggles again.)* It's so assfuck beautiful here, Sterling. I was looking up at the sky and thinking about how much I don't want to go home and this cloud came over and it looked *exactly* like you — I'm not kidding, it was like, *exactly* your profile, and the second I had that frot — "frot"? — *thought,* your nose exploded and became this — I don't know, a flower or whatever, not a flower but just like … bits of cloud — it was like the cloud was offended that I thought you two looked exactly alike. *(Giggling.)* How does that make you feel?
STERLING. Um …
BECKY. *(Seeing the plates.)* Oooohh … dinner!
STERLING. Yes, Sonia made a salad before she left and I just —
BECKY. — Blowjob salad? *(This catches Sterling totally off guard. He chuckles. Becky giggles.)*
STERLING. Are you OK?
BECKY. Yes. No. *(She tosses the foliage off the porch.)* Yup.
STERLING. *(Eyeing her suspiciously.)* OK, so there's blowjob salad

and then I made a very special dish I call Chicken Los Angeles for your —
BECKY. — For my final meal, you can say it. Before I take my ... how many steps is it? *(Sterling just watches. What's going on with her?)* When they're taking you to the electric chair, it's a certain number of steps, right?
STERLING. It's probably different depending on where you're —
BECKY. — What would be your laff meal? Jesus — *last* meal.
STERLING. I've never thought about it.
BECKY. Oh, come on. You'd have a burger, wouldn't you? All you vegetarians would. You'd have a big, fat, juicy-ass, bloody, veiny burger. *(Giggling.)* Come on, admit it. With bacon! Double bacon cheese. And don't say you've lost your taste for meat because that is *(Highly pitched.)* bullshiiiiiiiiit.
STERLING. Fine, I'd get a hamburger.
BECKY. I knew it! *(She takes a bite of Chicken Los Angeles.)* Mm ... this is really good. It looks like my guts, but seriously, it's good.
STERLING. Thank you. Are you up for making some smoothies after dinner?
BECKY. *(Proudly.)* Did it. Made 'em this afternoon. Final meal smoothies. They're in the fridge, in the Tupperware bowl.
STERLING. Oh, I didn't see it ... *(He starts to get up. She pulls him back down.)*
BECKY. I'll get 'em. You just rest your pretty li'l face. *(She pokes his cheek, then scampers off to the kitchen to pour the smoothies. From the kitchen.)* So what'd you do all afternoon? *(Mocking him.)* Read, walk, build trails ...
STERLING. I've decided to put in an outdoor shower so I planned that out.
BECKY. Cool. Where's it gonna be?
STERLING. Outside the bathroom, I think. I'm not completely sure.
BECKY. Is it gonna have walls?
STERLING. Not walls exactly but ... I think I'm gonna do, sort of, woven sticks and things.
BECKY. Whoa ... Nature Master. *(Sterling chuckles.)* Aww ... I don't wanna leave. *(Genuinely sad about this.)* We don't even get to have a Sunday together!
STERLING. I know.

BECKY. Although I guess your Sundays are kinda like your Mondays.
STERLING. Kind of. *(Becky brings out the drinks.)*
BECKY. *Salud.*
STERLING. *Salud. (They drink.)* Whoa ... rum.
BECKY. Yeah, I figured it's my last night so ... might as well be "binge night," right? Seeing as we won't be smoking a bowl together. *(Sterling smiles nervously.)* Jesus, Ster-fry, I'm kidding. Have you always been so uptight?
STERLING. Yes.
BECKY. Even when you were a kid?
STERLING. Yes.
BECKY. Jesus. Did Grampa and Gramma like, beat you or something?
STERLING. Not exactly ... *(Sterling takes a tiny sip of smoothie. It's way too strong for him. He puts it down. Becky looks up into the tree. Sterling notices the dirt on her shirt.)*
BECKY. Come out, parrot! Where is he?
STERLING. It's late for them. You've got some dirt on your shoulder.
BECKY. Oh ... *(She brushes at it.)*
STERLING. Here. *(He starts to brush it off. He sees that her whole back is covered in the reddish dirt.)* My God ... you're filthy. *(Becky giggles.)* Did you fall down?
BECKY. Sort of. Not exactly.
STERLING. What happened?
BECKY. Um ... I laid down. I went off the lower lower trail, down to the river. I mean, I guess that's what you mean by "the river" — it's not much of a river, but anyway. I laid down and looked up at the clouds and, I told you, that's when I saw your profile for a second and ... I didn't exactly ask God to kill me but I just said ... well the thing is, since I don't believe in God, I had to use your God, so I laid down and said out loud, "Sterling's God, if you feel that it's the right time to take my, Becky Thurman's, life, please take this opportunity to send a coral snake to come and bite me, preferably near a vein so it won't take too long." And then I just laid there like that and waited for about an hour, maybe more, I don't know — *(Annoyed.)* I never know what time it is here. About halfway through, I realized I shouldn't have said that stuff out loud, I should've just thought it, because the vibrations of my voice probly scared off all the coral

snakes. Oh, and I brought your rum bottle with me — *I'm telling you,* because I know you want to *know* whenever alcohol's involved. I figured alcohol thins out your blood so if God did want me to get bitten, it'd kill me faster because it wouldn't take as long to get to my heart. Maybe that's not how it works — I don't know, I got a D in biology. So anyway, when nothing happened, I just came back up here. *(Beat.)* So that's why I'm so dirty.
STERLING. That was incredibly stupid.
BECKY. Fuck off, you're not me.
STERLING. Becky, what would've happened if you'd … I mean, what would I have done? It would've taken hours to find you, first of all —
BECKY. — Yeah, you probly wouldn't have found me. And if you had, you'd have called the helicopter and I would've died before it got here.
STERLING. So you want to die? That's what you're telling me?
BECKY. No, meathead, you're missing the whole point. I was just giving God the opportunity to take me if that was his wish and apparently it wasn't. It was a spiritual moment, Sterling — I was talking to God. I thought you, of all people, would appreciate that. *(Silence.)* You're really pissed at me, aren't you? *(Nothing from Sterling. Loudly.)* You're. Really. Pissed at me. Aren't you? Do you have a fucking emotion left in your body or did you leave those in America too?
STERLING. *(Furious.)* Yes! Yes, I do. And you mean "The United States" because this is called America too and yes, I am really fucking pissed at you, Becky.
BECKY. Good! I would be too. *(Getting up.)* I'm gonna go change my shirt. *(She goes into the bedroom.)* By the way, I left the empty rum bottle down at the river, by mistake. I'm sure Hector will find it in like two years. Yeah, I would be royally fucking pissed at me if I were you.
STERLING. *(Shouting towards the bedroom.)* So that's why you did it, to make me angry?
BECKY. No. It's not all about you — I told you why I did it. I was talking to God.
STERLING. I don't … *(Stopping himself. Becky comes out in a clean T-shirt.)*
BECKY. You don't what, Sterling? Jesus, would it kill you to finish a sentence? I don't think you've finished a single sentence since I've been here.

STERLING. I don't understand why you would do something like that.
BECKY. Well, there's plenty I don't understand about you too.
STERLING. *(Angrily.)* Like what? *(Beat.)* Like what?
BECKY. I don't know. I didn't like, have an example in mind — I just said it. *(Beat.)* Alright, I don't understand why you'd just give up on everything?
STERLING. I didn't give up.
BECKY. You moved to the fucking jungle! How is that not giving up?
STERLING. Why is building a life here *not as good* as building a life in the States? It doesn't matter where you are. Either way, you just have all this time to fill and —
BECKY. — Bullshit! You're not building a life here, you're getting blowjobs from your cleaning lady. There's no one here, Sterling. Have you noticed? *(Yelling.)* Hullo?? Is anyone here?? *(No answer.)* See? No one.
STERLING. I made a radical change in my life. That doesn't mean I'm — [giving up.]
BECKY. — Listen to you. You're exactly like my mom. You both take facts that are like, obvious to everyone around you and you twist them and make it sound like there's no other choice besides whatever fucked up choice you made.
STERLING. I don't think I do that. I don't think your mother does that either.
BECKY. Yes, she does.
STERLING. *(Angrily.)* I have great respect for your mother. I love her.
BECKY. Well if you love her, why'd you disappear to Costa Rica for the rest of your life? You were acquitted, dude — who cares where your "vacation money" came from, it's over. And who gives a shit what my dad thinks, or Karen. You're handsome, you're funny, you're like the smartest guy I've ever met, you speak a bazillion languages … Fuck Karen. When you came over and had fondue with us, I just remember Karen being a royal cunt to you all weekend and not letting you open your mouth without telling you how stupid you were.
STERLING. I'm finding it hard to take advice about not giving up, from someone who just tried to get bitten by a coral snake.
BECKY. Oh grow up — I wasn't trying to get bitten. *(Beat.)* Shit, I have to call my dad. You were supposed to remind me.

STERLING. Now?
BECKY. No, yesterday. His birthday was *yesterday*. *(Getting up.)* Shit. I am the worst daughter … We're two hours behind East Coast, right?
STERLING. One.
BECKY. OK, so that means it's like *(Grabbing Sterling's wrist and checking his watch.)* 7:45 there? Ughk, I'm such a loser. I should try him — where's the phone? *(Searching for it.)*
STERLING. There's no signal.
BECKY. I'll go up the hill.
STERLING. There's no signal up there.
BECKY. Still?
STERLING. Yeah, it's still out.
BECKY. You tried today?
STERLING. No, but …
BECKY. Then how do you know?
STERLING. It stays out for a few days.
BECKY. *(Finding the phone, heading out.)* I'm gonna go try.
STERLING. It won't work.
BECKY. Whatever, maybe it'll work for me.
STERLING. Marybeth is dead. *(Becky just stares at him.)*
BECKY. How do you know?
STERLING. Your mother said.
BECKY. You called her?
STERLING. She called.
BECKY. While I was down at the river?
STERLING. Monday. She left a message on Monday night.
BECKY. *(Confused.)* But I got here on Monday … *(Pause.)* She's been dead all week? You've known all week?
STERLING. Yes. *(She stares at him in disbelief.)* I tried to tell you … I was going to tell you on Tuesday when you came up to the labyrinth but you'd just seen the anteater and you were so excited and … I thought I'd wait a little and then … I couldn't. I wanted you to relax and … get away from everything. I wanted you to have this week — I haven't seen you in … *(Beat.)* The signal *does* go in and out here and your mother knows that sometimes there's no way to reach me for days so … I haven't called her back yet.
BECKY. *(Like a ghost.)* Marybeth. *(Long pause.)* I'm going to prison.
STERLING. You're not —
BECKY. — I'm going to prison.

STERLING. It was an accident — they never should've told you you might —
BECKY. — You have no idea, Sterling.
STERLING. Becky, I'm a lawyer. You're seventeen, it was an accident. You're not going to prison. *(She starts walking toward the bedroom.)* Where are you going? Will you please leave the door open? *(Becky walks directly into Sterling's bedroom door, slamming her forehead into the wood. Sterling races over to her, touches her head, checks the wound. She leans in and kisses him on the lips, barely. Stunned, he pulls away. He tries to give her a parental embrace. He can vocalize all this if it helps: "whoa! ... shhh ... it's OK, it's OK." Becky pulls away.)*
BECKY. I was there, in Jessie's dad's office with Marybeth. I wasn't having sex with Tyler. He wanted me to but he was really drunk and I didn't feel like it. Tanya thought it'd be really funny to get a video of Marybeth jumping into the pool with her wings on. We told Marybeth over and over exactly what it was gonna be like and she said she really wanted to do it. We said, all you have to do is stand up there, flap your wings, and jump. We even made her practice the jump a couple times off the bottom stairs. Jessie's brother had a flag of Maryland hanging up in his room so he got it and we tied it to Marybeth's belt loop, in the back, so it looked like she had a tail. We were planning on having people underneath her, between the pool and the house, holding out quilts just in case she didn't jump out far enough. But she didn't wait for us to get ready. She just got right up on the windowsill and jumped. I wasn't fixing her wing, like they said, I was trying to grab her arm and pull her back in, and I wasn't laughing, I was saying, "Marybeth, don't go yet." That's the truth. I promise. Then she just — it was like she had a death wish or something — she just ... went. It was the most horrible sound I've ever heard, when she hit the ground. It just went crunch. It was the same noise as when you forget you have your headphones on and you take a bite of cereal. And that was it. Then it was just, like, people screaming and everybody running for their cars. Everyone was trying to pull out as fast as they could but they were all blocking each other so someone would pull out a little ways and then honk and then ... Tyler was the first one out. Tanya put a quilt over Marybeth and then called the ambulance. After they came and took Marybeth away, Tanya went over to the video camera on the lawn and opened it up but the tape was gone. I'm pretty sure Tyler took it. I knew Marybeth was gonna die right then and there. I knew even before she hit the ground. I

probly deserve to die too or at least go to prison but I swear to God, Sterling ... I never meant to ... everyone was laughing at her and yes, she looked ridiculous, but when it was just me and her in that office ... she was *so* happy. She was just ... happy. She was grabbing onto my arm and laughing and saying, "My wings, Becky! Look, my pretty wings, Becky! Look, my pretty wings, Becky." *(She's crying now. Sterling watches her. He goes over to the shelf, removes a wire basket, and drops it onto the floor with a* clank. *He kneels, and dumps out its contents. Locks of various types, twelve or so, clatter onto the floor. He goes to work arranging them. He's making a mini floor plan of his house, a guide: which locks go with which doors and windows. They are marked with colored tape. When they're all laid out, he selects one, and brings it over to the kitchen window.)*
STERLING. Can I get a hand, please? *(Becky, confused, gets up and joins him at the window. Re: the shutter.)* I just need you to lift that up — watch your fingers. These can be finicky so we should do them tonight. Sonia can clean out the fridge ... *(He pulls the shutter closed and locks it.).*
BECKY. What are you doing?
STERLING. I'm coming with you.
BECKY. No, you're not.
STERLING. I am.
BECKY. Sterling ... [don't.]
STERLING. We just have to lock up.
BECKY. Thank you, but don't.
STERLING. I am.
BECKY. Seriously ... don't.
STERLING. I should be there. For you and your mom. *(Pause. Becky knows he won't change his mind. She feels some relief.)*
BECKY. My dad's gonna love that.
STERLING. Your dad's gonna deal with it. We'll catch the plane to San Jose together. Hector and I will put the front doors on in the morning. *(Beat.)* What do you feel like doing?
BECKY. Smoking a bowl. *(Beat. He goes over to his bookshelf and removes a book. He sits down next to Becky. He opens the book. Inside is a pipe and weed in a plastic baggy. He does what needs to be done, hands the pipe to Becky. She takes a hit. She hands it to him. He takes a hit. He offers her another but she refuses.)* That's all I want. *(He nods. He sets the pipe down. Becky fishes a piece of paper out of her pocket and hands it to him.)*

STERLING. What's this?
BECKY. I was gonna read it to you during our final meal. Now it's sort of too late. It's that poem I wrote about you and Karen. It's stupid. Here.
STERLING. Will you read it to me? *(She thinks it over. She doesn't like the idea. She unfolds the poem, stares at it, then ...)*
BECKY. *(Reading.)* Poem number nine: Sterling Bremen and Karen McKinney

> How 'bout those Oysters?
> One Saturday evening over cheese lava, jean jackets,
> embroidery, stubble, Vivaldi, Chubby Hubby ice cream,
> and a joke about how fat our dog Mandy's getting,
> you promised me and Jenna
> that after you visited the Queen
> and saw her diamonds go by on a conveyor belt
> like at a billionaire's grocery store, you said
> (and I laughed the hardest)
> you'd take us to Cape Cod,
> to a shack called Peggy and Pete's
> for Oysters that me and Jenna couldn't possibly
> say were disgusting.
> We didn't believe you because all Oysters are like mucus.
> That was seven years and two months and a week ago.
> How 'bout those Oysters?

(She folds up the paper and starts to put it back in her pocket.)
STERLING. Can I have that? *(She hands it to him. Pause.)*
BECKY. Can I ask you a favor?
STERLING. Sure.
BECKY. Don't say no, OK?
STERLING. OK.
BECKY. Can we please go do the labyrinth?
STERLING. What, now?
BECKY. Yeah.
STERLING. It's pitch black.
BECKY. You said you do it at night sometimes.
STERLING. Only when there's a full moon.
BECKY. Please?
STERLING. Alright. *(He gets up, goes to the drawer, gets the flashlights.)*
STERLING. Do you want red or blue?

BECKY. I don't care, it's gonna be pitch black.
STERLING. You get red then.
BECKY. OK. Red. *(She takes the flashlight.)* What's out there now?
STERLING. What do you mean?
BECKY. I mean, like … animals.
STERLING. I don't know. Let's go see. *(He turns on his flashlight. She turns on hers. They stand there for a moment, scared of what'll happen when they go outside. Sounds of the jungle at night. Lights fade to black. Then … flashlights out.)*

End of Play

PROPERTY LIST

Book
Backpack
Frozen fruit in baggies
Coconut syrup
Blender
2 tall glasses
Smoothies
Package of digestive biscuits
Pen
Chapstick
Trendy music gadget, earphones
2 mugs
Water carton
Broom
2 place settings
Pebble
Tropical foliage
Wristwatch
Wire basket with locks and colored duct tape
Hollowed-out book
Pipe, baggy with marijuana
Paper
Flashlights, red and blue

SOUND EFFECTS

Bird call
Howler monkey in distance
Scratching on tin roof
Loud frantic scratching
Jungle at night

NEW PLAYS

★ MOTHERHOOD OUT LOUD by Leslie Ayvazian, Brooke Berman, David Cale, Jessica Goldberg, Beth Henley, Lameece Issaq, Claire LaZebnik, Lisa Loomer, Michele Lowe, Marco Pennette, Theresa Rebeck, Luanne Rice, Annie Weisman and Cheryl L. West, conceived by Susan R. Rose and Joan Stein. When entrusting the subject of motherhood to such a dazzling collection of celebrated American writers, what results is a joyous, moving, hilarious, and altogether thrilling theatrical event. "Never fails to strike both the funny bone and the heart." –*BackStage*. "Packed with wisdom, laughter, and plenty of wry surprises." –*TheaterMania*. [1M, 3W] ISBN: 978-0-8222-2589-8

★ COCK by Mike Bartlett. When John takes a break from his boyfriend, he accidentally meets the girl of his dreams. Filled with guilt and indecision, he decides there is only one way to straighten this out. "[A] brilliant and blackly hilarious feat of provocation." –*Independent*. "A smart, prickly and rewarding view of sexual and emotional confusion." –*Evening Standard*. [3M, 1W] ISBN: 978-0-8222-2766-3

★ F. Scott Fitzgerald's THE GREAT GATSBY adapted for the stage by Simon Levy. Jay Gatsby, a self-made millionaire, passionately pursues the elusive Daisy Buchanan. Nick Carraway, a young newcomer to Long Island, is drawn into their world of obsession, greed and danger. "Levy's combination of narration, dialogue and action delivers most of what is best in the novel." –*Seattle Post-Intelligencer*. "A beautifully crafted interpretation of the 1925 novel which defined the Jazz Age." –*London Free Press*. [5M, 4W] ISBN: 978-0-8222-2727-4

★ LONELY, I'M NOT by Paul Weitz. At an age when most people are discovering what they want to do with their lives, Porter has been married and divorced, earned seven figures as a corporate "ninja," and had a nervous breakdown. It's been four years since he's had a job or a date, and he's decided to give life another shot. "Critic's pick!" –*NY Times*. "An enjoyable ride." –*NY Daily News*. [3M, 3W] ISBN: 978-0-8222-2734-2

★ ASUNCION by Jesse Eisenberg. Edgar and Vinny are not racist. In fact, Edgar maintains a blog condemning American imperialism, and Vinny is three-quarters into a Ph.D. in Black Studies. When Asuncion becomes their new roommate, the boys have a perfect opportunity to demonstrate how open-minded they truly are. "Mr. Eisenberg writes lively dialogue that strikes plenty of comic sparks." –*NY Times*. "An almost ridiculously enjoyable portrait of slacker trauma among would-be intellectuals." –*Newsday*. [2M, 2W] ISBN: 978-0-8222-2630-7

DRAMATISTS PLAY SERVICE, INC.
440 Park Avenue South, New York, NY 10016   212-683-8960   Fax 212-213-1539
postmaster@dramatists.com   www.dramatists.com

NEW PLAYS

★ **THE PICTURE OF DORIAN GRAY by Roberto Aguirre-Sacasa, based on the novel by Oscar Wilde.** Preternaturally handsome Dorian Gray has his portrait painted by his college classmate Basil Hallwood. When their mutual friend Henry Wotton offers to include it in a show, Dorian makes a fateful wish—that his portrait should grow old instead of him—and strikes an unspeakable bargain with the devil. [5M, 2W] ISBN: 978-0-8222-2590-4

★ **THE LYONS by Nicky Silver.** As Ben Lyons lies dying, it becomes clear that he and his wife have been at war for many years, and his impending demise has brought no relief. When they're joined by their children all efforts at a sentimental goodbye to the dying patriarch are soon abandoned. "Hilariously frank, clear-sighted, compassionate and forgiving." –*NY Times.* "Mordant, dark and rich." –*Associated Press.* [3M, 3W] ISBN: 978-0-8222-2659-8

★ **STANDING ON CEREMONY by Mo Gaffney, Jordan Harrison, Moisés Kaufman, Neil LaBute, Wendy MacLeod, José Rivera, Paul Rudnick, and Doug Wright, conceived by Brian Shnipper.** Witty, warm and occasionally wacky, these plays are vows to the blessings of equality, the universal challenges of relationships and the often hilarious power of love. "CEREMONY puts a human face on a hot-button issue and delivers laughter and tears rather than propaganda." –*BackStage.* [3M, 3W] ISBN: 978-0-8222-2654-3

★ **ONE ARM by Moisés Kaufman, based on the short story and screenplay by Tennessee Williams.** Ollie joins the Navy and becomes the lightweight boxing champion of the Pacific Fleet. Soon after, he loses his arm in a car accident, and he turns to hustling to survive. "[A] fast, fierce, brutally beautiful stage adaptation." –*NY Magazine.* "A fascinatingly lurid, provocative and fatalistic piece of theater." –*Variety.* [7M, 1W] ISBN: 978-0-8222-2564-5

★ **AN ILIAD by Lisa Peterson and Denis O'Hare.** A modern-day retelling of Homer's classic. Poetry and humor, the ancient tale of the Trojan War and the modern world collide in this captivating theatrical experience. "Shocking, glorious, primal and deeply satisfying." –*Time Out NY.* "Explosive, altogether breathtaking." –*Chicago Sun-Times.* [1M] ISBN: 978-0-8222-2687-1

★ **THE COLUMNIST by David Auburn.** At the height of the Cold War, Joe Alsop is the nation's most influential journalist, beloved, feared and courted by the Washington world. But as the '60s dawn and America undergoes dizzying change, the intense political dramas Joe is embroiled in become deeply personal as well. "Intensely satisfying." –*Bloomberg News.* [5M, 2W] ISBN: 978-0-8222-2699-4

DRAMATISTS PLAY SERVICE, INC.
440 Park Avenue South, New York, NY 10016 212-683-8960 Fax 212-213-1539
postmaster@dramatists.com www.dramatists.com

NEW PLAYS

★ **BENGAL TIGER AT THE BAGHDAD ZOO by Rajiv Joseph.** The lives of two American Marines and an Iraqi translator are forever changed by an encounter with a quick-witted tiger who haunts the streets of war-torn Baghdad. "[A] boldly imagined, harrowing and surprisingly funny drama." –*NY Times.* "Tragic yet darkly comic and highly imaginative." –*CurtainUp.* [5M, 2W] ISBN: 978-0-8222-2565-2

★ **THE PITMEN PAINTERS by Lee Hall, inspired by a book by William Feaver.** Based on the triumphant true story, a group of British miners discover a new way to express themselves and unexpectedly become art-world sensations. "Excitingly ambiguous, in-the-moment theater." –*NY Times.* "Heartfelt, moving and deeply politicized." –*Chicago Tribune.* [5M, 2W] ISBN: 978-0-8222-2507-2

★ **RELATIVELY SPEAKING by Ethan Coen, Elaine May and Woody Allen.** In TALKING CURE, Ethan Coen uncovers the sort of insanity that can only come from family. Elaine May explores the hilarity of passing in GEORGE IS DEAD. In HONEYMOON MOTEL, Woody Allen invites you to the sort of wedding day you won't forget. "Firecracker funny." –*NY Times.* "A rollicking good time." –*New Yorker.* [8M, 7W] ISBN: 978-0-8222-2394-8

★ **SONS OF THE PROPHET by Stephen Karam.** If to live is to suffer, then Joseph Douaihy is more alive than most. With unexplained chronic pain and the fate of his reeling family on his shoulders, Joseph's health, sanity, and insurance premium are on the line. "Explosively funny." –*NY Times.* "At once deep, deft and beautifully made." –*New Yorker.* [5M, 3W] ISBN: 978-0-8222-2597-3

★ **THE MOUNTAINTOP by Katori Hall.** A gripping reimagination of events the night before the assassination of the civil rights leader Dr. Martin Luther King, Jr. "An ominous electricity crackles through the opening moments." –*NY Times.* "[A] thrilling, wild, provocative flight of magical realism." –*Associated Press.* "Crackles with theatricality and a humanity more moving than sainthood." –*NY Newsday.* [1M, 1W] ISBN: 978-0-8222-2603-1

★ **ALL NEW PEOPLE by Zach Braff.** Charlie is 35, heartbroken, and just wants some time away from the rest of the world. Long Beach Island seems to be the perfect escape until his solitude is interrupted by a motley parade of misfits who show up and change his plans. "Consistently and sometimes sensationally funny." –*NY Times.* "A morbidly funny play about the trendy new existential condition of being young, adorable, and miserable." –*Variety.* [2M, 2W] ISBN: 978-0-8222-2562-1

DRAMATISTS PLAY SERVICE, INC.
440 Park Avenue South, New York, NY 10016 212-683-8960 Fax 212-213-1539
postmaster@dramatists.com www.dramatists.com

NEW PLAYS

★ **CLYBOURNE PARK by Bruce Norris.** WINNER OF THE 2011 PULITZER PRIZE AND 2012 TONY AWARD. Act One takes place in 1959 as community leaders try to stop the sale of a home to a black family. Act Two is set in the same house in the present day as the now predominantly African-American neighborhood battles to hold its ground. "Vital, sharp-witted and ferociously smart." –*NY Times*. "A theatrical treasure…Indisputably, uproariously funny." –*Entertainment Weekly*. [4M, 3W] ISBN: 978-0-8222-2697-0

★ **WATER BY THE SPOONFUL by Quiara Alegría Hudes.** WINNER OF THE 2012 PULITZER PRIZE. A Puerto Rican veteran is surrounded by the North Philadelphia demons he tried to escape in the service. "This is a very funny, warm, and yes uplifting play." –*Hartford Courant*. "The play is a combination poem, prayer and app on how to cope in an age of uncertainty, speed and chaos." –*Variety*. [4M, 3W] ISBN: 978-0-8222-2716-8

★ **RED by John Logan.** WINNER OF THE 2010 TONY AWARD. Mark Rothko has just landed the biggest commission in the history of modern art. But when his young assistant, Ken, gains the confidence to challenge him, Rothko faces the agonizing possibility that his crowning achievement could also become his undoing. "Intense and exciting." –*NY Times*. "Smart, eloquent entertainment." –*New Yorker*. [2M] ISBN: 978-0-8222-2483-9

★ **VENUS IN FUR by David Ives.** Thomas, a beleaguered playwright/director, is desperate to find an actress to play Vanda, the female lead in his adaptation of the classic sadomasochistic tale *Venus in Fur*. "Ninety minutes of good, kinky fun." –*NY Times*. "A fast-paced journey into one man's entrapment by a clever, vengeful female." –*Associated Press*. [1M, 1W] ISBN: 978-0-8222-2603-1

★ **OTHER DESERT CITIES by Jon Robin Baitz.** Brooke returns home to Palm Springs after a six-year absence and announces that she is about to publish a memoir dredging up a pivotal and tragic event in the family's history—a wound they don't want reopened. "Leaves you feeling both moved and gratifyingly sated." –*NY Times*. "A genuine pleasure." –*NY Post*. [2M, 3W] ISBN: 978-0-8222-2605-5

★ **TRIBES by Nina Raine.** Billy was born deaf into a hearing family and adapts brilliantly to his family's unconventional ways, but it's not until he meets Sylvia, a young woman on the brink of deafness, that he finally understands what it means to be understood. "A smart, lively play." –*NY Times*. "[A] bright and boldly provocative drama." –*Associated Press*. [3M, 2W] ISBN: 978-0-8222-2751-9

DRAMATISTS PLAY SERVICE, INC.
440 Park Avenue South, New York, NY 10016 212-683-8960 Fax 212-213-1539
postmaster@dramatists.com   www.dramatists.com